NIGGER

A DIVINE ORIGIN

By

Shaba Shabaka

And

Dr. Ernie A. Smith
Special Linguistic Consultant

Milligan Books   **California**

Published and Distributed by:
Milligan Books, Inc.

Cover Design by
ClearVision Communications/A3Arts.com

Formatting by
Alpha Desktop Publishing

First Printing, October 2003
10987654321

ISBN 0-9742811-5-8

Milligan Books, Inc.
1425 W. Manchester Ave., Suite C
Los Angeles, California 90047
www.milliganbooks.com
E-mail: drrosie@aol.com
(323) 750-3592

DEDICATION

In Memory of Chief John Kinsey
And
Sister Sandra Davis

CONTENTS

Acknowledgments v
About The Author- Dr. Ernie A. Smith vi
About The Author- Shaba Shabaka viii
Foreword.. ix
Introduction.. xi
Chapter 1   What Is In A Name?.................................... 1
Chapter 2 The Origin And True Meaning Of
The Word Nigger 5
Chapter 3 NGR In The Ancient MDW NTR 11
Chapter 4 The God Ngers and The Goddess
Neggur (Hathor)... 18
Chapter 5 The Goddess Ninkhursag (Neggur)
and The God Ningirus.. 25
Chapter 6 Nigritian Traditions, Languages, and Culture 31
Chapter 7 Aryan's Introduction To The Root Word 'NGR' .. 39
Chapter 8 The Nickname Negro 45
Chapter 9 Nigritude 49
       I President And Poet Leopold Sedar Senghor
       II W.E.B. Du Bois
Chapter 10 The 'N' Word.. 59
Bibliography 70
Illustration Acknowledgments... 74

ACKNOWLEDGMENTS

Acknowledgment must be given, first and foremost, to the Creator and Ancestors, without whom this work would not have come into fruition.

Special thanks to Derotha Williams for reviewing and editing my manuscript.

I owe a large debt of gratitude to the late Chief John Kinsey, whose pioneering efforts and research on this topic served as a springboard for my quest to pursue this topic further and produce this book.

A special acknowledgment and memorial to the late Sandy Davis, who was one of my strongest and staunchest supporters during this endeavor.

I also give special thanks to Gloria Williams Mitchell and all of my family members for their unwavering support and encouragement while working on this publication.

ABOUT THE AUTHOR

Dr. Ernie A. Smith was born September 7, 1938, in Haskel, Oklahoma. His elementary school education began at Paul Lawrence Dunbar Elementary School in Tulsa, Oklahoma. In 1949, his family moved to Los Angeles, California, and there in the urban inner city schools of Los Angeles, he received his entire secondary education.

Ernie Smith received his high school diploma from John C. Fremont High School in Los Angeles in 1957. In June of 1962, he received his Associate of Arts Degree from Los Angeles Metropolitan College of Business; and as a Junior College transfer student, in September 1962, he enrolled at California State University at Los Angeles (CSULA).

In June 1967, Ernie Smith received his Bachelor of Arts Degree from Cal State University L.A. For two years following his graduation, he worked in telecommunications as an assistant producer at KTTV studios in Los Angeles. As fortune would have it, in 1970, while working evenings as a volunteer at Operation Bootstrap, a South Central Los Angeles Community Social Service Organization, he was recruited, admitted, and began post-baccalaureate studies, in the School of Social Sciences, at the University of California at Irvine. In 1974, Ernie Smith received his Ph.D. Degree, in Comparative Culture, from the University of California at Irvine, and thus embarked full time upon a university teaching career

As an interdisciplinary scholar, Dr. Smith has conducted research and published works in several behavioral and social science disciplines and taught a variety of behavioral science, humanities and social science courses. Until 1982, Dr. Smith was a Full Professor of Linguistics, in the Department of Linguistics, at California State University at Fullerton. Since then, as a career shift, Dr. Smith Has pursued postgraduate studies and conducted research in bio-medical ethics, informed consent and ethno-gerontology. Currently, Dr. Smith is a Professor of Medicine, ethno-gerontology and Clinical Linguistics in the Department of Internal Medicine, at the Charles R. Drew University of Medicine and Science.

ABOUT THE AUTHOR

Shaba Shabaka, a.k.a. Jurline Woolen, was born and reared in La Grange, Texas. She made her home in Los Angeles, California. She owned and operated Shabben, a popular art store, for the purpose of offering black art at affordable prices to the Black community. She was a strong advocate on issues concerning the Black community and an active member of the Black Community Education Task Force.

Ms. Shabaka spent many years researching the history of Ancient Nigritia, known today as the continent of Africa. She was a founding member and president of the Nigritian Commission—an organization initiated to trace the history and heritage of black culture. She hosted the former television show "Nigritian Insights."

Ms. Shabaka successfully authored several small books, the most notable being tilted "Nigritia," which was published in 1992. Just as her present and final book "Nigger - A Divine Origin" was being published, she transitioned to join the ancestors following a long battle with breast cancer. She will be remembered and heralded for her perseverance in swimming against the current in an attempt to spawn new revelations and conceptions about a controversial and touchy subject, namely the "N" word. Her lasting legacy, however, will be the raising of black consciousness, dignity, and pride in reconstructing segments of our history that for centuries have been lost, hidden, distorted, or in some instances outright stolen.

FOREWORD

The 'N' word continues to be the most controversial, despised, and misused word in the English language. Because it was used predominantly as part of the white establishment's arsenal to dehumanize and debase people of African descent, the term is popularly viewed as being offensive, derogatory, and vulgar. Many Blacks cringe when they hear the word and many would like to have it removed entirely from dictionaries. Because the term is a hot seat of contention and generates strong negative reactions, a public 'slip of the tongue' in the work place or in the media could cause one to be reprimanded, demoted, fired, or sued. Political careers could also be compromised.

In spite of the prevailing views surrounding the use of the 'N' word, many Black comedians regularly use the term in their comic routines. The Black hip-hop generation also use the term prolifically in their rap music and as a term of endearment when referring to close friends. Even so, they are not so accepting of the term being used by non-Blacks. It is still off limits to white rappers such as Eminem and Latino entertainers like Jennifer Lopez, who caused a public outcry by using the 'N' word in her lyrics. The big question is "Why is it o.k. for Blacks to use the 'N' word and not others"?

Amidst this controversial dialogue, the author Shaba Shabaka introduces a surprising and enlightening point of view on the origin of the 'N' word. Hers is an historical look at the divine Kemetic (Egyptian) origin of the word! She has researched the hieroglyphic writings and other historical texts as well as incorporated empirical linguistic evidence to support her thesis. As fate would have it, the youth of our Black hip-hop generation have intuitively embraced the 'N' word and been using it positively without having a conscious knowledge of it's divine origin. Could it be that they are merely acting as a conduit through which the original divine power of the word 'Nigger' can emerge and proliferate?

Derotha Williams

INTRODUCTION

This book is about the origin and true meaning of the word Nigger. In this book Sister Shaba Shabaka rejects the thesis that the origin of the so-called 'N' word is the Latin word *Niger*. Sister Shaba Shabaka maintains that, while the word nigger may have entered into the English language via the Latin or Romance languages, the French word being *negre,* the Spanish and Portuguese word being *Negro;* the issue is, was there an origin of the word nigger before it entered into the Latin language?

As Chairwoman of the Nigritian Commission, Sister Shaba felt it was incumbent upon her to write this book. Sister Shaba makes no claim that she is a linguist or scholar of the ancient Kemitic sacred writings properly known as the Medu Neter (MDW NTR) but commonly called Hieroglyphics by so-called Egyptologists. She contends that the empirical evidence which she presents to support her thesis is irrefutable. Making note of the fact that even modern lexicographers of English dictionaries admit that as a Latin word, the origin of the word *niger* is unknown, Sister Shaba traces the root meaning of the word *niger* to the ancient MDW NTR. She then critically examines the meaning of the word nigger in the ancient Kemitic language and the fact that phonetically the word is the name of both an ancient Kemitic or Egyptian God and Goddess. Having its roots in the name of ancient Kemitic or Egyptian deities, Sister Shaba posits the so-called 'N' word as having a divine origin.

Sister Shaba then examines the belief system of the ancient Kemitic people who she calls Nigritians. She contends that the land of ancient Kemit or Egypt was also the home of people who viewed themselves as being and called themselves Ngrs. In her examination of the belief system of the ancient Nigritic people, Sister Shaba poses the question what is in a name? She then argues that unlike their descendants in the diasporas today, the ancient Nigritic people believed there is power in a name. Sister Shaba explores the white supremacists notion that to be viewed as, to be called or to refer to ones self as a nigger is something negative. She then examines the hostility that exists between some descendants of the ancient land of Kemit over the usage and acceptance of the 'N' word by those who call themselves Nigritic or Nigritians. Nigritians are extremely proud of their ancient ancestors. They view descendants of enslaved Nigritians in America, who are ashamed of their Nigritian heritage, as pathetic souls.

Chapter One

WHAT IS IN A NAME?

One may ask what is in a name? I maintain that power is in a name. In ancient Nigritic (Egyptian) history, the tradition regarding naming a child was incorporated into the single deity who was invoked (Barnes 1982:48). Each child was named after a deity. They believed that the deity for whom the child was named was present at the conception and responsible for the successful birth, development, and the destiny of the child. According to Barnes in his book The Conception of God in Ancient Egypt (1982:48)

> "When devising a name of a child, an Egyptian had in mind a particular one among the many `deities. It is quite possible that when he composed a name all divinity—the entire extent of divine action—was incorporated in the single deity who was invoked ... But it is also conceivable that the name giver wanted to leave undefined which of the innumerable deities was responsible for the successful birth and development of the child."

It is said that at the time of birth, the Goddess Hathor (Neggur) shoots lunar rays into the child to

1

give it a spiritual soul. An ancient tradition that lives on in some Nigritian cultures is the rite of passage which connects the child to its birth spirit. In this rite of passage the child is ritually taken out to face the midnight skies, in an outreached position to face the heavens. (see Roots, Alex Haley) It is said that at this precise time the child is connecting to the ruling planetary spirit of the universe, its guardian spirit and birth spirit.

In Ancient Nigritic Egyptian culture, the secret name embodying the soul of a child was mother given. (Barbara Walker 1982:709) Each child was given a dual name. One was spiritual and the other was physical. The spiritual name was known only to a few. It was considered part of the soul, which was sacred. Even today, the spiritual body is known as the inner being. It is the seer of the consciousness that comprehends the true, the beautiful and the righteous. It is the consciousness of joy and bliss. Here lies the majestic seat of the human will. The spiritual body is the Seat of the Divine. Therefore, in the ancient Nigritic (Egyptian) culture, a spiritual name was a carefully kept secret. "On the other hand, a man or god could be cursed if his secret magical name was learned by an enemy and spoken in the wrong context." (Walker, B., 1982:710) Thus, if known by evil forces, one could be influenced magically. By pronouncing the secret magical name under proper circumstances, one could be influenced for good or evil.

The physical or public name was that which referred to the physical body. The physical body is what an individual sees. It is the flesh, the tangible you. The name that you use generally is what is applied to the physical body. The way you walk, talk, and sleep is descriptive of your physical body. The activities through which you exert yourself daily are part of that recognizable body. Your family, friends and peers judge you by your physical characteristics.

Again I will ask, what is in a name? Power is in a name. The ancient Phoenicians kept the name of their deity a secret. This is attested in the New Larousse Encyclopedia of Mythology (1968:80):

> "The real name of the divinity was almost never known. As in Israel, one avoided pronouncing it, though perhaps for different reasons. In Phoenicia, the object was to prevent strangers from discovering it lest, in turn, they invoked the god, drew his benevolence upon themselves, and succeeded by diverting his interest in turning him from his own people".

According to the New Age Bible Interpretation Old Testament Volume III, The Egyptian God 'Ra' had several secret names, one of which was the essence of his power: The New Age Bible states (1955:100:101):

> "Ra's Secret name was hidden in his breast, but Isis, by strategy and with the aid of the serpent, secured possession of it, the Name passing from Ra's breast to her own. Then because she knew the name, she was able to restore life to the dismembered body of Osiris. Ra's secret Name was the very essence of his power."

3

Nigritian people in the diaspora have suffered a similar fate to Osiris. Through the horrors of captivity and enslavement, Nigritian ancestors were dismembered from the motherland Nigritia (Africa). They were for "three centuries physically and more seriously, spiritually, cut off from the source which, for four million years, had nourished and informed their ancestors:" (Senghor, L.S, Black World 1971:13) Like the body of Osiris, they were scattered to many European nations. Many were shipped to British colonies which later became the United States. After chattel slavery was abolished in 1865, Nigritians remained in a subtle form of captivity, both mentally and physically. The United States government sanctioned the oppression and suppression of Nigritians. Under laws written by United States officials, Nigritians were denied their civil rights and basic human rights.

Through all the horrors that have happened to Nigritians, their royal, regal and divine (NGR) ancestral name was almost misplaced. Knowledge of their ancestral Nigger gods (Neggur and N-ger-s) was almost forgotten. As in ancient Egypt, with the knowledge of the Egyptian God Ra's secret name, the Goddess Isis was able to put the God Orisis' body back together. I maintain that it will be through the Nigritian people's knowledge of their ancient history, and of self that we will put the word Nigger and Nigritian history in proper perspective. Remember, to know a thing or a person's real name is to know its power. "To pronounce it correctly is to free its energy." To deny your real name is to deny your power and energy." (unknown)

Chapter Two

THE ORIGIN AND TRUE
MEANING OF THE WORD NIGGER

When the meaning of the word nigger is sought in modern English dictionaries; without exception, one will find all definitions provided associating the word nigger with Black or African people and the etymology of the word traced ultimately to Latin. Merriam Webster's Collegiate Dictionary states (1993:785).

> "Nigger \'nigar\ n [alter. of earlier *neger*, fr. MF *negre*, fr Sp or Pg *negro*, fr. *negro* black, fr. L niger] 1700 1: a black person – usu. taken to be offensive 2: a member of any dark skinned race – usu. taken to be offensive. 3: a member of a socially disadvantaged class of persons"

The definition of nigger provided in the American Heritage Dictionary is as follows (1976:887)

> "Nigger: (*nigar*) n. *Vulgar*. A Negro or member of any dark skinned people. An offensive term used derogatorily. [Earlier English dialectal *neeger, neger,* from French

5

negre, From Spanish n*egro, NEGRO].*" 1:
a person of – usu. taken to be offensive 2:
a member of any dark skinned race. –
usu. taken to be offensive. 3: a member of
a socially disadvantaged class of persons."

Thus we find that as the etymology given in both
of these dictionaries of the English language the word
nigger is traced to the Latin word *niger,* via the
French word *negre* and the Spanish and Portuguese
word *negro.*

Notice that these dictionaries say that the Latin
'niger' is also the root origin of the Negro which
entered the English language via Spanish and
Portuguese. When we explore the meaning of the word
in Webster's Collegiate Dictionary, the definition of
the word 'negro' is given as (1993:777):

\ˋne- (,)gro\ *n. pl* Negroes. [Sp. or Pg. Fr.
negro black, fr. L *nigr, niger*] (1555) 1: a
member of the black race dis-tinguished
from members of other races by usu.
inherited physical and physiological
characteristics without regard to language or culture; esp: a member of a
people belonging to the African branch of
the black race – sometimes taken to be
offensive 2: a person of Negro descent –
sometimes taken to be offensive – Negro
adj. – Negro-ness.

The American Heritage Dictionary's definition of
the word 'negro' is given as:

6

> Negro (ne'gro) n. pl – groes. 1. A member of the Negroid ethnic division of the human species, especially one of various peoples of central and southern Africa. 2. A descendant of these or other Negroid peoples. See Negroid. – *adj.* 1. Of, pertaining to, denoting, or characteristic of a Negro or Negroes. 2. Negroid (see). [Spanish and Portuguese *negro*. A Negro, "black," from Latin *niger*, black. See niger in Appendix .

As stated above, in all of these dialects or varieties of the Latin or Romance languages the ultimate source or language base given as the etymological origin for the words 'nigger' and "Negro" is the Latin word 'niger'. However, the American Heritage Dictionary directs the reader to 'see the word niger in the appendix'. In the Appendix of the American Heritage Dictionary we find the following concerning the word niger

> [niger. Black. Latin adjective of unknown origin. NEGRO, NEILLO, NIGRESCENCE, NIGRIFY, NIGRITUDE, DENIGRATE, NECROMACY, NIGROSINE.]

Here then is the crux of the issue. The lexicographers who compiled the American Heritage Dictionary openly concede that the language base or etymology, i.e., root word from which the word Niger is derived into Latin, is "unknown" to them. This in itself reveals that the word niger was not originally a Latin word but rather, a word that was adopted or 'borrowed' into

Latin from another language. I maintain that while the English language lexicographers may not be willing to, or do not feel obliged to delve beyond Latin or the Romance languages for the origin and true meaning of the word nigger, given the significance that this word has as an appellation of offense and yet a term of endearment among many people of Niger-Congo African ancestry, it is incumbent on scholars of Niger-Congo African or Nigritic descent to pierce the Euro-centric veil of secrecy.

In an effort to do so, I have examined the sacred writings of the ancient people of Kemit for a possible answer. As a result of my studies, I contend that the word nigger is not derived originally from Latin, an Indo-European language. But rather, the origin and true meaning of the word nigger is found in the language of the Nigritic people who inhabited the ancient land of Kemit (Egypt). I maintain that while the word nigger has a negative connotation in some European dictionaries and among many descendants of enslaved Niger-Congo African people today; long before the word nigger became part of the European lexicon, the root word niger was in usage in ancient Kemit dating back to at least 4000 BC. I maintain that, by using the recognized method of comparative philology and etymology, when a careful and critical analysis is made of the word nigger, consistently one will find the word identifying ancient gods and goddesses of Kemit (Egypt) as well as people who viewed themselves as Nigritic or Nigritian people. That is, whether on the continent of so-called Africa, the Indian sub-continent of Asia, the so-called Middle East of Syria and Arabia and even in the Western

Hemisphere of what is today known as the West Indies and the Americas, the word nigger can be traced to many ancient civilizations.

Chapter Three

NGR IN THE ANCIENT MDW NTR

Written on temples and pyramids for thousands of years *the root word NGR* is found in antiquity throughout the land of ancient Egypt or Kemit. The root word NGR is written in ancient Egyptian or Kemitic hieroglyphics.

But in order to understand the ancient Kemitic origin of the word nigger as being from the Kemitic root NGR, it must be understood that the ancient writing system used by the people of ancient Kemit did not entail the use of vowels. As Sir E.A. Wallis Budge explains (1978:lviii)

> "The whole question of the use of separate vowels which we find in Egyptian words is one of considerable difficulty, and it seems to me quite clear from statements that are made on the subject by Egyptologists that no one has yet succeeded in solving the problem. It seems quite obvious that the scribes systematically wrote certain words without vowels and expected the reader to supply them"

11

As an attestation of what Budge posits here, in his text <u>Egyptian Hieroglyphs</u> Samuel Mercer states (1993:5):

> "8. Groups of consonants, e.g. sdm, htp, ntr, are made pronounceable by the insertion of a short e` between the letters. Thus we read these words; sedem, hetep, neter. But, the e`, it must be remembered, is quite conventional. It is not at all represented in the hieroglyphs. 9. There are no written vowels in Egyptian..."

As a third attestation that the sacred writings of the ancient people of Kemit did not contain vowels, in his text <u>Egyptian Grammar</u> Alan H. Gardiner states (1927:7)

> "7. Vowels not written. In reading the last section, the student has doubtless noted that the sound-values derived from the ideogram of the 'mouth' (*ra*) and from the ideogram of the 'house' (*par*), were said to be not *ra* and *par*, but simply the consonantal elements entering into those two words, namely *r* and *p+ r*. To put it differently, the Egyptian scribes ignored the vowels in writing. It thus came about that both these signs could be used in a far greater number of different words than might otherwise have been the case".

Clearly based on what has been shown here, the words Medu Neter would be written mdu or mdw ntr.

12

This prompts the question what exactly is the meaning of the words mdw ntr. According to Budge in his text <u>The Rosetta Stone</u> (1989: 174) "The Egyptians believed that hieroglyphic writing was invented by the god Thoth". In his <u>Egyptian Hieroglyphic Dictionary</u> (1978:402) Budge states that the words 'neter metut' or 'metut neter' means "the words of the god [Thoth] any book or inscription written in hieroglyphs".

As an attestation that the ancient Kemitic or Egyptian people believed it was the god "Thoth" who gave man the power of speech, W.V. Davies states in his text: <u>Egyptian Hieroglyphics</u> (1987:4) "The Hieroglyphic script was always more than just a writing system. The Egyptians referred to it as 'writing of the divine words', or simply as 'divine words". In this same work W.V. Davies also states (page 38) "Hieroglyphic writing was traditionally regarded by them as the invention of the gods, in particular of Thoth the divine scribe, who was often referred to in texts as 'the lord of writing'. Davies states (1987: 36,42) that the word *mdw* means (speak) the word *ntrw* means 'gods' and the word *ntrwt* means 'goddesses'. Davies posits the words *ntr nfr* as meaning 'good god' (Davies 1987:44,45).

According to Budge in his work entitled <u>First Steps In Egyptian</u> (1972: 303, 304) the word 'metu' means both 'words', and 'speech' and the word 'neter' means both 'god' and 'divine'. I should state here that, based on these findings, henceforth in this work when the words 'mdw ntr' are used, I am referring not only to the divine or sacred writings of the ancient Kemitic people, but also to the speech of the ancient people of Kemit as well.

I maintain that, in the ancient Kemitic language, it is *the root* word NGR *that is* the true origin and etymology of the word *Niger*. *I maintain further that* just as the ancient Kemitic root words *mdw ntr* have a divine origin and meaning, the root word NGR also has a divine origin and meaning. Firstly, in that according to Budge (1978:348), in the ancient Kemitic language the letter 'n + i' or 'ni' means 'belonging to' and the letters g + r or gir mean 'the throne'. The tri-consonant root of the word nigir being NGR, this yields the expression 'belonging to the throne'.

According to Budge's hieroglyphic dictionary (1978:1004) the word Niu means the Equatorial Lakes. Budges's dictionary states that the word `qer-t' means 'hollow, carven, cave source of the Nile' (Budge, 1978:774b). Budge states that the words Qerti Qerti refers to "the two caverns in the first Cataract out of which the Nile was believed to rise" (see p775a). When the word 'Niu' (the Equatorial Lakes) is added as a prefix to the word 'qer-t' (the source of the Nile) this yields 'Equatorial Lakes, source of the Nile'. When the word 'Ni' (belonging to) is added as a prefix to the word 'qer-t' (source of the Nile) this yields the compound or word Ni-qerti which means 'belonging to the source of the Nile'.

The point I am making is that the original homeland of the people who were known as NGRS was the 'Equatorial Lakes source of the Nile', the Southern source of the Nile being Lake Victoria in Uganda where it flows North and junctures with the Blue and white Niles in Sudan, then on into the Mediterranean in Egypt. The source of 'Blue Nile' being Lake Tana in

14

Ethiopia where it flows North West to Khartoum in Sudan, the source of the 'White Nile' is "Lake No" in South Central Sudan where it flows North to Khartoum. I maintain that the people who are the NGRS of West and Niger-Congo Africa or Nigritia have their historical origins or roots in and are descended from the NGRS of Eastern Nigritia or ancient Kemit (Egypt).

Evidence of the cultural and linguistic ties between the Eastern and Western NGR people is provided by Gerald Massy in his text <u>A Book Of The Beginnings</u> (1974) Massey states (1974:610)

> "The Babwende, whose territory on the Kongo is far away down towards the Atlantic ocean, have a typical term for a river, or *the* river: it is NJARI. That is the original for the name of the NILE. The word is formed from ARU or ARI, the river, with the definite plural article NAI prefixed. NAIARI is the Nile at the waters, not merely a river. The j may represent the k in the earlier KARUA, whence the form NACHAR or NACHAL, the Nile, in Aethiopic. In the African Nalu dialect, NUAL is the type-name for water.

As further evidence that there are cultural and linguistic ties between the NGRS of Eastern and Western Nigritia (Africa), Massy cites the fact that the Nile and the Niger rivers are derived from the same root word Quorra.

"The river Niger is also known by the native name of the QUORRA. Karua (Eg) means the lake as a source; and Ni, or in the full form NNI, is the flood or inundation. It can be shown that this Ni represents the Egyptian Nun, because in the Bright of Benin the Niger is called the Nun or Nin, as in the Benin. Thus, the name of Niger in full is NUN-QUORRA, and Nun-Karua (Eg) is the flood from the lake. Benin in Egyptian would read, the place of inundation, or the flood of fresh water."

As further support for my contention here, according to the comparative and clinical linguist Ernie Smith (1999) the letters /K/ and /Q/ represent sounds that are produced by the same, or very closely the same, articulation. The same organs being involved in the production of the sounds represented by the letter /k/ and /q/, the letter /k/ and /q/ represent sounds that are homorganic consonants. Since the letters /k/ and /q/ are interchangeable for the same sounds, this means the word nkr and nqr are the same sounds. According to Smith, the letter /k/ and /g/ also represents the homorganic consonants. Being produced by the same articulation, the difference in the sounds represented by the letter /k/ and /g/ is in the manner of their production—not in the place. According to Smith, in phonetics the sound represented by the letter /k/ is called a 'voiceless dorso-velar stop'. The sound represented by the letter /g/ is called a 'voiced dorso-velar stop. In other words, the place of articulation of the sounds represented by the letter /k/

16

and /g/ is the same but the manner in which they are produced is different. In the case of the sound represented by the letter /k/, as the air stream goes through the glottis (the space between the vocal cords) the vocal cords are not tightened. As a result, the air stream is not obstructed and the sound is not voiced. On the other hand, in the case of the sound represented by the letter /g/, the vocal cords are tightened as the air goes through the glottis. As a result, the sound represented by the letter /g/ is voiced. As such the letter /k/ and /q/ represent voiceless dorso-velar stops and the letter /g/ represents a voice dorso-velar stop.

The purpose of the preceding discussion of the articulatory definition of the speech sounds represented by the letters /k/, /q/ and /g/ is to establish that in the ancient Kemitic or Egyptian language the words 'nkr', 'nqr' and 'ngr' would have been very close in their pronunciation. Based on the fact that there were different regional dialects of the ancient Kemitic (Egyptian) language, the word 'nigger' would have been pronounced somewhat differently in different dialects. It is well known that the ancient Egyptians used the existence of homophones in their language (i.e., words that sounded the same but meant something different) to write words using the rebus or sharade principle.

17

Chapter Four

THE GOD NGERS AND THE GODDESS NEGGUR (HATHOR)

As I have shown, the root word NGR existed in the ancient Egyptian sacred writings or hieroglyphics, i.e., the mdw ntr. It is attested as being in the mdw ntr 4000 years before any evidence of a Latin civilization even existed. Therefore, the Latin language could not be the language base of the word *niger* or *ngr*. Comes now my evidence that the root word NGR has a "divine" origin and meaning.

As I have stated above, in the ancient Kemitic language the word for god was the triconsonant 'ntr'. However, according to Samuel Birch in his text <u>The Egyptian Hieroglyphs,</u> (1857) in Egyptian hieroglyphic writing the G/J/and T are interchangeable. Specifically Birch states (1857:240)

> "There are certain distinctions, too, here to be observed: the B sound has been in many Coptic words replaced by *v*, *f*, or *u*, the A by *e*, *o*, *ou*, or *oo*; the H and U, too, seem to have been equivalent, and the G, J and T are represented by the same hieroglyph."

18

Thus, we see that in ancient Kemitic writing the letters G, J, and T, were interchangeable. Given this fact, I maintain that the word NGR could also appear in the Egyptian Hieroglyphics with the spelling NJR or NTR. In other words, the words NeGeR and NeJeR and NeTeR are merely three ways of spelling the word 'God". I maintain that the root word NGR was not only a way of spelling the word 'god,' the root word Ngr was the name of a specific male god whose name was N-ger-s and a goddess whose name was Neggur. As empirical evidence and attestation of the existence of the word Ngr as the name of the gods N-ger-s and Neggur in the language of the ancient Kemitic (Egyptian) people I cite Budge's Egyptian Hieroglyphic Dictionary (1978:341) See Table 1 below.

Thus, according to Budge the word 'N-ger-s' refers to the god of the 8th Aat. The Goddess Neggur is one of the oldest female deities of ancient Kemit. According to Walker, the word Neggur is a title of Hathor in her guise as the "Goose who laid the Golden Egg" (sun). (See Walker, letter 1991 in appendix). As an attestation that the Goddess 'Neggur' is the "goose goddess who laid the golden egg", in his Egyptian Hieroglyphic

Dictionary, Sir E.A. Wallis Budge defines the word 'Neggur' as follows (1978:398):

Negg-ur 〰 ⚬⚬ 🦆 ⚬ 🧍 〰 ⚬⚬ ⌣ ⚬ 🧍, B.D. 59, 3, the goose-goddess who laid the sun-egg.

Thus, the fact is, thousands of years before the composition of the book of Genesis in the Holy Bible, the Kemitic goddess Hathor (Neggur) was worshipped as a goddess in many lands. In fact the ancient Kemitic people believed the goddess Hathor (Neggur) existed even before creation. According to Barbara Walker (1983:374) "brought forth in primeval time herself, never having been created" the Goddess Hathor "was the mother of every god and goddess".

I reason that, if the Goddess Hathor created the universe and all that it contained, the goddess Hathor created the earth, the moon, the sun and all the planets in the universe. This means that Hathor created all the rivers, lakes, seas, and all forms of water on earth. I reason that, if it is from Hathor or the goddess Neggur's black cosmic womb that all forms of life come, then, it is the goddess Hathor (Neggur) who created the first human beings. If the Goddess Hathor created the first human beings, while it may have been the God 'Thoth' or 'Djehuti' who endowed humans with speech, it was the divine Goddess Hathor or Neggur who gave to her human creation the anatomical equipment or organs, i.e., capacity for speech.

20

The Goddess Hathor is often seen with braided hair dangling from her head. She is also seen as a cow-headed sacred animal or as a cow headed Goddess. She is frequently represented with a woman's face, and cow's ears.

Sometimes she is given a human head adorned with a horned headdress with the solar disk and the uraeus. Sometimes she is represented as a full figured woman dressed in embroidered gowns but always with her headdress. According to Gay Robins in her text <u>Women In Ancient Egypt,</u> (1993:142)

> "In the Old Kingdom a large number of high class women were priestesses (hemet Netjer) of Hathor. *Hemet Netjer* is the feminine form of a common male title *hem netjer* which denotes a particular type of priest within the temple hierarchy".

Great ceremonies were held in Hathor's temple. Priestesses organized and took part in temple ceremonies. "In the old period, noble ladies frequently bore priestly titles; they were usually prophetesses of Neith or Hathor." (The New International Encyclopedia, Volume 19, 1923:201)

The Goddess Hathor (Neggur) is the Lady of the Sycamore tree. She hides in the foliage of the tree and appears to the dead with bread and water of welcome. It was she, they believe, who held the ladder by which the deserving could climb to heaven. She would personally carry them to safety on her back to the after life.

There were great holidays celebrated in honor of the Goddess Hathor (Neggur). One such holiday is the New Year's great celebration. This is the anniversary of the Goddess Hathor's (Neggur) birth. Before dawn, priestesses would bring Hathor's image out on the terrace to expose it to the rays of the rising sun. (New Larousse Encyclopedia 1968:25) The celebration would begin and last for days. There was dancing, music, and many other activities. It was a great celebration. There were many festivals held in honor of Goddess Hathor, some in the spring and autumn.

The Goddess Hathor's legacy and origin go beyond ancient Egypt. Some historians trace the tradition of the Goddess Hathor (Neggur) from the land southeast of Egypt, called the land of Punt. According to Sergen Hable Sellassie, <u>Ancient And Medieval History To 1270</u> (1972:24)

> "Parallel to Punt we find another term which is very often used in Egyptian hieroglyphics: Ta Neter The Land of God. The origin of this term is obscure. According to the old tradition, Punt was believed to be the original abode of the Gods and from there they traveled to the Nile valley where they finally settled."

According to Galbraith Welch in his book <u>North Africa Prelude, The First Seven Thousand Years</u> the location of the land of Punt is Somalia.

The legacy of the Goddess Hathor (Neggur) and the root word NGR is not confined to Egypt. The Goddess traditions and spiritual beliefs are found in

22

various civilizations. Many of her traditions have been adopted by traditional religion in many parts the world today.

According to Ivan Van Sertima in his book <u>Black Women In Antiquity</u> (1990) there was a shrine built in honor of the Goddess Hathor in the Phoenician City of Byblos. In fact, Van Sertima states (1990:81,82) "She was the chief deity here and was widely known as the Lady of Bablos. This data is indicative of the extremely close Egypto/Phoenician relationship." According to the <u>New Larousse Encyclopedia of Mythology</u>, (1987:449) in the Pantheon of Oceania, we find the root word NGR is associated with a god or deity. Firstly, there is the very commonly known Polynesian God Tangaroa. Under the heading Complexity of the Pantheon of Oceania the <u>New Larousse Encyclopedia of Mythology</u> states

"It is very hard to give a general view of this pantheon of Oceania. It is quite possible to extract from travelers' books a long list of divinities, for instance Polynesia Tangaroa, Tane, Rongo, Tu, and a host of other deities, some of whom turn up in a more or less large number of islands or archipelagos, either with the same name invariants of dialect, such as Tangaros, Kanaloa, Taaroa, or with more or less synonymous names, or with approximate or identical attributes. Thus the chief Polynesian god Tangaroa, is found in Micronesia under the more abstract name of Tabu-reiki (the sacred chief)..."

Clearly the root word NGR is found in the name of the chief Polynesian god Tangaroa. Since most of the people of the Polynesian islands, Somoans, Hawaiians, Tongoans, Papuaians, etc. are kinky haired people who very much resemble the Nigritian people of ancient so called Africa, there should be no question as to whether or not these people are NGRS.

Chapter Five

THE GODDESS NINKHURSAG (NEGGUR) AND THE GOD NINGIRUS

In ancient Mesopotamia (Babylon) we find the root word NGR in the names of an ancient Goddess (Ninkhursag) and an ancient God (Ningirus). The Goddess Ninkhursag or (Ninghur-sag) (nkrsg) is a name for the "Lady of the Great Mountain." (New Larousse Encyclopedia of Mythology, 1968:55) Some historians compare the Goddess Ninkhursag to her counter part Goddess Hathor. According to Barbara Walker:

> "She was the createss of the first human beings, whom she made out of clay, a special magic later copied by the biblical God. She is associated with sacred serpents. Like her Egyptian counterpart Hathor, she sometimes appears a divine cow. "Holy milk" from temple dairy farms at Lagash nurtured Assyrian kings five thousand years ago. Many Mesopotamian kings included among their qualifications

for the thong the assertion that they had been fed with the holy milk of Ninhursag. Calves were sacrificed to her, in the role of first born."

"The Todes of Southern India still sacrifice a calf to the Cow Mother who represented the earth, with a prayer that includes the word Ninkurshag. They say the origin of word is unknown, but it is a very holy word." (Walker, B. 1983:728)

In his work <u>Babylonian Life And History,</u> Sir E.A.Wallis Budge states that the Goddess Ninkharsag created gods and goddesses to aid her in healing the sick. Budge states, (1975:215,216):

"Goddess Ninkharsag and the eight gods whom she created to heal special diseases, taught the use of medicines and the manner of applying them to men. Other gods of medicine were Ninurta and his wife Gula, and Ninaza, the patron of physicians, and his son Ningishzidia. The symbol of this last named god was a round staff with a double-sexed, two-headed serpent called Sachan which was coiled, and a form of this is the recognized mark of the craft of the physician at the present day (visual 12). The serpent was chosen as the symbol of renewed youth and immortality because it cast its skin and so renewed its youth, and because it cast its longevity."

26

Like her counter part the Goddess Hathor (Neggur), Ninkhursag (Ninghursag) is associated with sacred serpents and sometimes appears as a divine cow. According to the New Larousse Encyclopedia (1968:56) the Goddess Ninkhursag (Ninghursag) sometimes bore the title 'Mother of the gods'. Thus, it follows that the Goddess Ninkhursag gave birth to the God Ningirus, (ngrs).

Patesi or the governor Gudea, also a priest of Lagash of Sumerian city-states built a temple in homage to God Ningirus. According to the New Larousse Encyclopedia (1968:53) in Babylon history the God Ningirus was believed to have created the universe. He is the god of the hunter, god of fields and canals, who brings fertility and life.

According to Sir E.A. Wallis Budge, in his work <u>Babylonian Life and History,</u> ancient writings from ancient Babylon state that King Urukagina, reigning about 2700 BC, called on God Ningirsus to help him to rule his people. He set out to stop the abuse that had been forced upon his people by the officials and the rich. He is known as "royal reformer." (Budge 1975:21) King Urukagina cut down on the numbers of officials and their privileges; and in turn he helped to rebuild the lives of the poor. He stopped priests and the rich from exploiting the poor. He set out to correct everything which was wrong and called on the God Ningirsus to aid him. He called on the God Ningirus to aid him in drawing up a code of laws which has much in common with the laws set out in the famous codes of (K) Hammurabi. In his book Babylonian Life and History (1975:21), Budge states that King Urukagina's

laws came much earlier than (K) Hammurabi's laws.
Like the ten commandments of Moses, King Urukagina's
laws were a gift from the god Ningirsus and heaven.
One of Babylon's ancient names is Ka-Di-Ngirri. The
root word NGR is found within this ancient name.
Budge states that, (1978:60)

> "The Sumerians called the city Ka
> Dingirra(ki),.*i.e.* the Gate of God, and
> TINTIRA, The Grove of Life. The
> Akkadians, i.e. the Semitic Babylonians,
> translated the old Sumerian name Ka
> Dingirra (Ki) by "Babilu, ... A name also
> meaning The Gate of God ...."

According to Gerald Massy, in his text <u>Book of
The Beginnings</u> Volume II. (1974), in the Assyrian
spiritual text we find God Ningar referred to as the
"pilot of heaven." Massey states that (1974:488.489)

> "In one of Akkadian magical texts the
> God Nin-gar is invoked, "Come, Nin-si-
> gar, great pilot of heaven, thrusting for-
> ward thy sublime tree, the lance." He is
> invoked in favour of the king, and in
> connection with one of the insignia of
> royalty, a weapon which causes terror,
> which wounds for majesty, the weapon
> which is raised, which projectile, by the
> side of majesty." Now as Nin-gar answers
> to the lord Har, pilot of the gods ...."

The New International Encyclopedia, (1927:479),
states that Amenemhet II, the son and successor of

Sesostris I, was responsible for a shrine to Hathor in Sinai, for Hathor is also known as the "Mistress of Mines." Clearly, as has been shown, the Goddess Hathor (Neggur) and the Ngrs (root word NGR) are found as the principal deities in many lands.

Chapter Six

NIGRITIAN TRADITIONS, LANGUAGES, AND CULTURE

As I have shown in chapter one, the existence of the word NGR in ancient Kemit language is recorded in stone. I maintain that, just as there are people today who worship Jesus Christ as their Lord and Savior, and as such call themselves Christians; in ancient Kemit there were people who worshipped the God Nger-s and the Goddess Neggur. As such, these people called themselves NGRS and were known as NGRS. I contend that, just as many of the people who lived in ancient Kemit were also known as Semitic people, those in ancient Kemit who worshiped the god NGRS were also called Nigritic people and were known as both Kemitic and Nigritic people.

That is, just as Christians who live in California are both Christians and Californians, the Nigritic people who lived in ancient Kemit were both Nigritic and Kemitic. As evidence of my contentions relative to the ancient Nigritic people in ancient Kemit, I cite the fact that monuments and temples that attest to their great achievements line the banks of the Nile. I maintain that through their monuments, statutes and names of their ancient deities, they speak from their graves. Nigritic features are chiseled and sculptured on polished marble and stones. Nigritic culture and history goes beyond what is known to us as history. In ancient civilizations, such as Ethiopia, Babylon and India, there were NGRS or Nigritic people who lit the torch of pre-civilization thousands of years ago. In Ethiopia they were called Nagran People. In Babylon they were called Ngirri people. In ancient India they were called Naga people. Nigritic culture had its beginning in the Stone Age; and today, the descendants of ancient Nigritic people inhabit the lands of Kemit (Egypt), Nubia (Sudan), Ethiopia, India, the Polynesian islands, as well as the North, the South and Central Americas.

In Central and West Africa there are two nations who proudly proclaim themselves to be Nigritic people. Namely Niger and Nigeria. But as I have shown, the fact is the descendants of ancient Nigritic people are currently found all over this planet.

Dr. William Smith, another great historian of Egyptian history and culture has examined the language of the ancient Egyptian people. His research into Egyptian and Nigritian history and culture is found in a four-volume set called Smith's Dictionary of the Bible, Volume I, II, III and IV. According to Smith, the ancient Egyptian language is one of the dialects of the great Nigritian family of languages. In volume I, Smith states (1981:675)

"The ancient Egyptian language, from the earliest period at which is known to us is an agglutinate monosyllabic form of speech. It is expressed by signs, which we call hieroglyphics. The language is compound: it consists of elements resembling those of Nigritian languages .... All those who have studied the African languages make a distinct family of several of those languages spoken in the northeast quarter of the continent, in which family they included the ancient Egyptian."

Today, there are linguists who concur with Dr. William Smith's finding. They support the scientific documentation that the ancient Kemitic (Egyptian) language is part of the great Niger-Congo African family of languages. Among these are the late professor Cheka Anta Diop, Dr. Ernie Smith, Dr. Asa Hillard, Dr. Molefi Asante, Dr. Theophile Obinga, and Dr. Samuel Caruthers to name but a few.

The point that must be made and clearly understood is that the ancient scribes of Kemit (Egypt) have recorded the invasion of ancient Kemit by many Caucasian nations. As a result, there were many non-Nigritic people who also inhabited ancient Kemit. Thus, it is important that a clear distinction be made as to who the Nigritic people of ancient Kemit were as oppose to those who were not Nigritic people, such as those who were Romans, Greeks, and Semites.

One of the ways that this can be done is the way the ancient scribes distinguished Nigritic from non-Nigritic people in their sacred writings.

When a careful examination is made of the pictogram writings of the ancient Kemitic scribes,

33

there will be quite evident physical and physiological differences that distinguish the people depicted. Some are painted black, some are painted red, some are painted brown and some are painted a yellowish beige. I maintain that the people who are depicted as black, red and brown are the Nigritic people. I maintain that besides skin color, there are also other natural biological features that physically and physiologically are more characteristic of Nigritic people, i.e., big thick lips, big broad noses, nappy or kinky hair.

When the sacred pictogram writings of the ancient scribes of Kemit are carefully examined, it will discern that there were people with elaborate braided hairstyles that are identical to the extremely popular braided hairstyles in Nigritic cultures in modern Africa and in the diasporas of the far East and Western Hemispheres. This ancient tradition in hair styling dates back to ancient Kemit and beyond. Indeed, on almost every pyramid and monument that depicts ancient Egyptians, whether on papyrus or chiseled on stone, Nigritic people are shown with elaborate braided hairstyles.

Kings, queens, pharaohs, women, men, boys, and girls wore braided hairstyles as well as priests, priestesses, commoners and others.

Today, Nigritic people wear braided hairstyles and this practice crosses status and class lines. Politicians, lawyers, doctors, famous movie stars, athletes, rich and poor, all wear braided hairstyles. The method and process of hair braiding used by the ancient Nigritic people over 4000 years BC (see visual) is still in place today. The Nigritic method of weaving an extension on to existing hair to create elegant hairstyles is still in use today.

I maintain that this Nigritian custom of braided hair has a divine origin as well. We find its roots in the spiritual practice of the Goddess Hathor (Neggur) and the Goddess Isis. One representation of Isis wearing braided hair is the sculpture of her nurturing the Christ child Horus from her left breast. The braid is symbolic of the great tree and its roots. The root of the tree is its source of life, which feeds her branches. Beads and berries have adorned Nigritian women's hair throughout history. In some Nigritian cultures it represented the commencement of a pregnancy. For example, in the Ashanti culture, where a pregnancy denotes a time for celebration women adorn their hair with beads even today. According to Gerald Massey in his text <u>Book of Beginnings, Volume II,</u> (1974:671)

> "When the Ashanti woman finds herself enceinte she not only put on her Gru Gru or beads or berries to show that the flower had set and seeded. She would go at once to the Oracle of the priest or priestess to have a spiritual consultation to obtain particulars from the (KLA) or tutelary Genus respecting the ancestors and future of the child."

Massey also states that the Goddess Isis wore beads to denote the child in the womb with which she was Guru. According to Massey (1975:671)

35

"The Gru-Gru worn by Isis denoted the other self, as the child in the womb with which she was GURU (Sansk.) The Gru Gru of beads or berries worn by the marriageable maiden signified the other second self of womanhood; the Gru-Gru worn by the Queens of Egypt in the shape of the vulture or the double Ureaus serpent was the crown of this second self duplicated in the maternal phase."

Throughout history, the land to the south of ancient Kemit was called "Punt" which is today called Somaliland or Somilia. The land of Punt was regarded by the ancient Kemites as "the land of the Gods" or as "God's Country." According to Galbraith Welch in his book, North African Prelude Years (1949:24, 25)

Punt (Somaliland) is the native country of the trees that yield the bulk of the frankincense used in modern commerce. It was the regio romataica of the Latins, because it produced such a profusion of aromatic plants. It was a land reputedly so delicious that sailors could steer towards it by the sense of smell alone — literally follow their noses. To the perfume — adorning Egyptians Punt was a place of mystic wonder. Its other name to them was "Gods Country": it was the place from whence in the old, old days they thought their ancestors had come."

There are other nations in Africa that state that they are descendants from the "gods." In the ancient Kemitic language the root word 'Ni' means "belonging

36

to" and the root 'GIR' means "the source". According to Budge, in the ancient Egyptian language the word 'ta' means "ground, land, earth, world soil; dust" (1978:815)". Budge states that the word 'Ta neter' means "Land of the God," the southern part of the Eastern Desert and Arabia" (1978:816). As previously referenced, Samuel Birch asserted that in the ancient Egyptian language, the letters G, J, and T are interchangeable. I maintain that the word 'Ta Negra' is merely a variant of the word 'Ta neter'. The words Ngers and Neggur being the names of two ancient Egyptian deities, in the ancient Egyptian language the word (Ta-NGR) "Ta neger' most certainly would mean "Land of the Gods."

Based on the fact that included in the meaning of the word Ta neter is the word 'world', this suggests that everywhere NGRs migrated to from their original homeland in Kemet (Egypt) they regarded the land they inhabited as being "Land cf the Gods." Thus NGR occupied lands would also be called Ta-NGR.

Evidence of this is that in every Nigritian diaspora the Nigritian people have kept many of the ancient NiGRitic ancestors' traditions alive. One notable example is the festivals that are held wherever there are Nigritians. In Brazil there is a great festival each year. In Cuba, New Orleans and the homeland (Nigeria) today called Africa there are great NGR festivals.

Chapter Seven

ARYAN'S INTRODUCTION TO THE ROOT WORD NGR

As I have stated in chapter one, many people believe the word nigger is a Latin word derived from the word *niger,* an adjective meaning *black.* However, as I have shown, being the names of Gods and Goddesses, the word NGR existed in the language of the ancient people of Kemit long before a Latin civilization even existed. Thus, the word *niger* is not of Indo-European or Latin origin.

According to Dr. J.B. Bury in his text <u>A History Of Greece To The Death Of Alexander The Great</u> (1917:94) in the territory just east of the ancient city of Thebes in southeastern Europe there was a city called "Tanagra". I have already shown that in the ancient Egyptian language the word 'Ta' means 'land' and that the root word 'NGR' means 'God'. I maintain that the people who the Greeks found in the land called Tanagra when they arrived were Nigritic people who had migrated there from ancient Egypt (Kemit). J.B. Bury states (1917:94)

> "The earliest colony founded by Greek sailors in the western seas was said to

have been Cyme on the coast of Campania. Tradition assigned to it an origin before 1000 B.C., a date which modern criticism has called in question .... Chalcis, Eretria, and Cyme ... join together, and enlisted for their expedition some Graeans who dwelled on the opposite mainland in the neighbourhood of Tanagra."

As I have shown in the beginning of this work, the origin of the word NGR is found in the ancient Egyptian language. The empirical evidence is that the root word NGR was introduced to Aryan or European people when they initially invaded and made contact with Negroid peoples (NGRs) of ancient India around 2000 – 1000 BC. According to Wallbank and Taylor in their book Civilization Past and Present (1942:72,73)

"We are ignorant of the history of India for a period of some five hundred years following the fall of the Indus valley civilization .... about 2000 B.C. however, tribes began to enter the land from the northwest .... We may conclude that the Hittites, Medes, Persians and Aryan-speaking tribes (called Indo-Aryans) which invaded India were branches of the great Indo-European family which probably had its original home somewhere near the Caspian Sea .... [p.73] The entire racial history of India is obscure. The Oldest remains go back to an early post-glacial period and seem to indicate a Negroid

40

stock akin to those of Africa. Various invasions into India of primitive Negroid stocks probably took place from time to time, and despite later invasions by Aryan-speaking groups from the north, the south lands of India even today possess remains of the ancient Indo-Negroid races. They have been called Dravidian because Dravida was the old name of the Tamil country."

Clearly here, Wallbank and Taylor posit the Dravidian people of ancient India as being a Negroid or NGR people and they posit these NGR people as being akin to the NGRs of Africa. According to Wallbank and Taylor, the Dravidian Negroid people of India possessed a civilization superior to that which the Aryans brought from the northwest (1942:73). Interestingly, besides the Dravidians, there were other NGR people the Aryans found in possession of the land of India when they arrived. These people were known as Nagas. Attesting to Wallbank and Taylor's finding that Negroid or NGR people occupied India before the Aryans arrived, in his book The Story Of Civilization: Our Oriental Heritage, Will Durant states (1954:396)

Among the Indus relics is a peculiar seal, composed of two serpent heads, which was the characteristic symbol of the oldest historic people of India—those serpent-worshiping Nagas whom the invading Aryans found in possession of the Northern provinces, and whose descendants still linger in the remoter hills.

41

Further South the land was occupied by a dark-skinned, broad-nosed people whom, without knowing the origin of the word, we call Dravidians. They were already a civilized people when the Aryans broke upon them; their adventurous merchants sailed the sea even to Sumeria and Babylon, and their cities knew many refinements and luxuries."

I maintain that is it not difficult to recognize the word Naga as the way many American and South African Aryans or Europeans pronounce the word NGR today. It is important to note here that the name of the characters used in Indian Sanskrit writing was originally called Nagari. Thus, it is not Sanskrit but the NGR alphabet that is traceable back to the oldest form of Indian writing. According to the International Encylopedia Volume VI (1922:736)

"Davanagari or Nagari. The name given to the characters in which Sanskrit is generally written, especially in northern and middle India. The Hindus commonly employ the second term rather than the first. The word *nagari* means "of the city, urban" (writing); *devanagari* signifies "(writing) of the divine city." As the Arab choreographer Albiruni in his account of India (about 1030 AD, trans. Sachau, i, 173) mentions a kind of writing called *Nagara* as in use in Malwa, whose chief city is Ujjain, it has been thought that the name of this script, *urban, urbane,*

> may possibly have some connection with King Vikrama's capital, which was a famous seat of learning and literature. The Nagari alphabet consists of 48 letters, and it is written from left to right. It is believed to have assumed its present characteristic form about the eighth century A.D., and, like the other Hindu scripts, it is traceable back to the oldest form of Indian alphabet ...."

Clearly in the word "Davanagari" and "Nagari" it is not difficult to discern the tri-consonant root NGR. What is even more important to note is that in the Hindu language, consistent with the divine origin of the word NGR, the word 'nagari' appended to the word "Dava" means "writing of the divine city." Thus, even in ancient India the root word NGR was originally associated with "God" and had a 'divine' meaning. It was in the European Persian language that word was corrupted and given a demonic connotation. According to the International Encylopedia Volume VI (1922:736)

> "DEV, dav, less accurately DEW, or DIV. The Persian word for demon, identical with Avestan *daeva*, and the same as Sanskrit *deva*, Avestan *daeva*, although the latter means "god" not "demon."

Chapter Eight

THE NICKNAME NEGRO

While there were many agencies that attempted to covertly disenfranchise Nigritians from their ancestral spiritual name NGR, I believe that more than any other agency, it was the Government of the United States of America that had the strongest influence in bringing this about. When the Federal Government applied the nickname 'Negro' as a racial category to identify Nigritian people, in the U.S. census the name 'Negro' became synonymous with Nigritian people as if it was an ancestral name. According to Hughes and Meltzer in their work <u>A Pictorial History of the Negro in America</u> (1966:2)

> "The Federal Government, through its agency, the United States Bureau of Census, has ruled that, in its official tabulation: A person of mixed white and Negro blood should be returned as a Negro no matter how small the percentage of Negro blood. Both black and mulatto persons are to be returned as a Negro without distinction. A person of mixed Indian and Negro blood should be

returned as a Negro, unless the Indian blood very definitely predominates and he is universally accepted in the community as an Indian. Mixtures of non-white races should be reported according to the race of the father except that Negro-Indian should be reported as Negro."

During the period when the word 'Negro' was used by the U.S. Census as a racial category, many descendants of enslaved Niger-Congo Africans (Nigritians) were not ashamed to use the word 'Negro' as their racial designation. However, during the 1960's, a movement spearheaded by the Nation of Islam (NOI) denounced the word 'Negro' as an appellation for the race of the Nigritic people. The basis for the NOI's rejection of the word Negro was that, the English language is a "bastard' language made up of words from many European languages. They argued that the word Negro was adopted into English from the Greek language. This contradicted the popular misconception posited in most English language dictionaries that the origin of the word Negro was of Latin origin.

One argument they made was that, if the word 'Negro' meant 'black' in Latin, French, Portuguese and Spanish languages, then descendants of enslaved Nigritians in America who did not speak these languages ought to called themselves 'black' in English which is the language they do in fact speak. However, having rejected the thesis that the word 'Negro' was of Latin origin, they maintained that the word "Negro" was actually derived from the Greek word 'nekro' or 'necro' which means 'dead'. They argued that, when the white man calls 'Black' people in America 'Negroes', he does so because he considers the 'Black' people in America to be mentally 'dead'.

Due largely to the influence of the NOI, the Black Nationalist Movement, and militant Civil Rights groups of the 1960's, when the word 'Negro' is used today among descendants of enslaved Niger-Congo Africans, it carries a negative connotation that is almost equal to that of the word 'nigger'. The difference is that, when the word Negro is used, images of slavery, human bondage, captivity, weakness, submission, subserviance to white oppression, a lack of self pride and hatred of ones own race are inferred.

Europeans conquered much of the known world. As conquerors, they rewrote history according to their interpretation. Some information passed down has been accurate and some has been inaccurate and extremely biased. In the American school system, most world history textbooks commence with Greek civilization. The ancient Nigritian Egyptians taught the Greeks. This part of history is ignored. Therefore, we do not get a complete and accurate history of the Nigritian people. I should mention here that, today there is actually a behavioral science field of study called "Negrology". The word 'negrology' was actually coined by Elijah Muhammad. It was used by the Nation of Islam (NOI) to refer to the Caucasian or white man's study of Nigritians and the breeding of certain types to be his lackeys and loyal sheepdogs. According to Dr. Ernie Smith, as defined by the Negrologists (scholars who study Negroes as traitors), Negrology is (1996) NEGROLOGY: 1. The Study of

NGRS (Niggers) or Negroes: Specifically the study of descendants of enslaved Niger-Congo Africans (Nigritians) whose reaction for-mation to the myth of white supremacy is; acquiescence, capitulation and opportunistic collaboration in the Caucasio-centric mental destruction and physical annihilation of Nigritian or Black people.

This definition of Negrology posits the study of Niggers (NGRS) as being exclusively the study of Negroes i.e., Nigritians who are called Negroes. Because this definition posits the study of NGRS as being the study of only a particular ilk of Nigritians, it is for this reason I reject this as an accurate definition of Negrology. The root word NGR is contained in the word Nigger, Niger and the word Negro. I believe that any definition of the word Negrology that tends to focus on the study of only one segment of the Nigritian people is misleading and creates confusion. The im-plication is that the study of NGRS is only about a form of mental illness among Nigritic people.

Chapter Nine

NIGRITUDE PRESIDENT AND POET LEOPOLD SEDAR SENGHOR AND W.E.B. DU BOIS

Webster's dictionary defines the word Negritude (Nigritude) as a consciousness of and pride in the cultural and physical aspects of the African heritage. In the sixties when most scholars, community leaders and politicians were expounding on a racial identity, of which would unite Nigritic people under one ancestral banner, Negritude was one of the words debated. It was on the fast track to become the vehicle, which would unite NGR people together under the banner of race in the U.S.A., Africa, Europe, Caribbean, Asia, West Indies and Middleast. As the word and philosophy of Negritude was forging ahead, there were entities at work to put a check on its success.

These entities were primarily European political leaders who set forces in motion to create doubt within the minds of some Nigritic people regarding the Negritude philosophy. Using the so-called educated Nigritic people, they were very successful in raising the question regarding the true meaning of the word 'Negritude' and sewing animosity between those enslaved by Anglo Europeans (Anglophiles) and those enslaved by the French (Francophiles).

According to President Leopold Senghor, there was a group of Nigritic scholars (Anglophiles) who were pushing for unity among NGRS hinged on an 'African personality' as opposed to skin color or melanin. These scholars rejected the words 'Negritude' and 'Nigritia' because they believed that in using these words they would be defining themselves according to the color of their skin. According to President Leopold Senghor (1971:8, 9)

"The English speaking Africans have asked us: "Why should you invent, in order to convey an idea which is dear to us all, a term which refers to color?" We reply that it is in conformity with the facts: with the laws of language and with ethnosocialogical realities. In nearly all the languages, the term indicating the civilization of a people refers to the country, the race or even the color of their skin. [p.9] "More important still, I know that our English-speaking brothers began by using the expression African Personality. This expression can only be translated in French by the word Africanite. It is the sum-total of the values of civilization of the African people. Now, to simplify the matter, these African people belong to two civilizations at least: the Arabo-Berber and the Negro African. It therefore results that the "African civilization"—in the unity of which Leo Frobenius believed strongly and even wrote a book with that title—has two

50

different faces of which it is a symbiosis. The African personality cannot then properly represent Negritude. If we want "to call a spade" we must like the Afro-Americans, use the term Blackness or Negroness."

It was then, primarily, the Francophiles i.e., the NGRS enslaved by the French who were not ashamed of being NGRS and using the word Negritude to unite all enslaved Nigritian peoples. While the English speaking African American Blacks were very vocal in their opposition to the word Nigritude, they were not opposed to the Nigritude philosophy. In fact, according to President Leopold Senghor, it was an African American scholar (W.E.B. Du Bois) who was the 'father of Nigritude as a crusade'. President Leopold states (1971:10)

"The dispute between Afro-Americans and Africans is less serious in spite of appearances. It truly amounts to a simple — both in time and in space. First, it derives from the fact that the common language used by the Blacks of the United States, on the one side, Blacks of the West Indies and of Africa on the other, facilitated understanding, hence the unity of action. Then, between the Afro-Americans and French speaking Africans, the French West Indies acted as a link. It was, thanks to Paulette Nardel, from Martinique founder of the Revue du Monde noir in the 30's, that I met Alain Locke and Mercer Cook; thanks to Guyana-born Leon Damas that I came across Langston Hughes and Countee Cullen. I met them but mostly read them. Thus, in its general meaning of discovery of black values and awareness, by the African American of his condition, Nigritude was born in the United States of America. The founders of Nigritude in French speaking countries always recognized this fact as Leon damas stated again last month in the March 18, 1971, issue of Jeune Afrique .... We must start with W.E.B Dubois who really was "the father of Nigritude as a crusade', as Lillian Kasteloot wrote, because he was the first person who thought of it in its totality and specificity, it aspects and aims, its objectives and means ...."

As stated earlier, whereas Black Americans rejected the word Negritude but accepted the ideology, there were black continental Africans from non English speaking countries and Arabs who rejected the Nigritude ideology. In fact, according to President Senghor, the Guineans and the Congolese were violently opposed to the Nigritude ideology. President Leopold states (1971: 17)

"Now let us examine the arguments put forward against Negritude by the politicians, starting from the interview of Leon Damas which I referred to earlier. This is the key question of that interview: "All critics of Negritude do not claim to belong to melanism, quite the contrary. Besides,

52

at the Algiers Festival, the attacks on Negritude apparently came from two sides: on the one side, from some Africans (Black) like the Guineans, the Congolese (Brazzaville) etc ...; on the other side from Arabs who saw in it an eventual factor of division of the continent. It is not really negative to insist on the color fact at a time when Africa is seeking its unity beyond its differences?" Here is the issue neatly raised. Let us see how. As far as the Arabs are concerned, they would be rather wrong to reproach the Blacks with cultivating their difference since they too did it before: first in the Nada movement (Renaissance) of Lebanese origin, then in present-day Arabism. On the other hand, to divide the African continent by means of language is slightly more positive than doing so by color. All the more so as none of the founders of Negritude even insisted on color but on race. Now, race, as we know, is not only the race with its physical qualities but also culture with its "values of civilization." Those values which the militants of Negritude have always praised. [p.18] It is most significant that it was the delegations of Guinea and Congo-Brazzaville that most violently attacked Nigritude.

President Leopold Senghor stressed the need for NGRS to have a racial identity. In his speech to the Organization of African Unity (OAU) in 1971 he said (1971:10)

53

"In our ideological struggle — for this is the heart of the matter-we need at once both the facts which only scientific research can provide, and the concepts which are the other instruments of dialectal reasoning. This is the reason why, far from stopping at Negritude or Negritie, we have taken up or launched: Negrie or Negrerie (the black community throughout the world). Negritie, or the old term Nigritia (the country of the Blacks), Negrism (the black ideology in the sense of subjective Negritude).

As has been shown, according Leopold Senghor, long before the Negritude movement emerged in the French speaking Nigritian diaspora during the 1930s and 1940s, W.E.B. Dubois had lunched the Niagara movement in 1905. The Nigritude ideology was designed to unite NGR people under certain great ideals and lines of policy. Some of the principles, upon which the Niagara Movement was founded, are set forth in its constitution. They are as follows:

a. Freedom of speech and criticism.
b. An unfettered and unsubsidized press.
c. Manhood suffrage.
d. The abolition of all caste distinctions based simply on race and color.
e. The recognition of the principle of human brotherhood as a practical present creed.
f. The recognition of the highest and best training as the monopoly of no class or race.
g. A belief in the dignity of labor.

h. United effort to realize these ideas under wise and courageous leadership.

During this time in history, Du Bois said that there were plans in the works to curtail the education opportunities of the colored children; "and while much is said about money-making, not enough is said about efficient, self-sacrificing toil and head and hand. Are not all these things worth striving for? *The Niagara Movement* proposes to gain these ends." (Du Bois, 1970:147) The Niagara Movement also laid out goals of which black men should try to achieve. They are as follows:

"To press the matter of stopping the curtailment of our political rights.

To urge Negroes to vote intelligently and effectively.

To push the matter of civil rights.

To organize business cooperation.

To build schoolhouses and increase the interest in education.

To open up new avenues of employment and strengthen our hold on the old.

To distribute tracts and information in regard to the laws of health.

To bring Negroes and labor unions into mutual understanding.

To study Negro history.

To increase the circulation of honest unsubsidized newspapers and periodicals.

To attack crime among us by all civilized agencies. In fact to do all in our power by word or deed to increase the efficiency of our race, the enjoyment of its manhood, rights and the performance of its just duties." (DuBois, 1970:147:148)

As we can see, the ongoing problems that Nigritic people are facing today, were addressed by Du Bois in 1905 and revisited by President Leopold Senghor and the Nigritude scholars in 1971. President Senghor states (1971:11):

> "For Du Bois, there is first, the condition of the Black in the U.S.A. There is the image the white man has of the Black, which portrays him as sub-human: a child-man, mindless and branded, whose intellectual and moral faculties have not yet developed and cannot develop at all. And that image filled the mind of the Black man himself. "It is a strange feeling," writes Du Bois about this "double consciousness, this impression of always looking at oneself through the eyes of others, of measuring one's soul to the scale of a world that looks at you with amusement, scorn and pity." (Black World, 1971:11)

W.E.B. Du Bois saw Negritude in it totality. The Niagara movement addressed the needs of Nigritic people as a nation. Du Bois laid out objectives and realistic goals for Nigritian people to achieve. For clarification, the words Nigritia and Negritude are not synomonous. The word Nigritia refers to a geographical location, the ancestral homeland of NGR people. The word Nigritude refers to an ideology or self awareness that exists in the minds of NGRs or Nigritian people. The late Chief John Kinsey said the word Nigritic refers to NGRs who don't know who they are. They have the same ancestry, culture, history, economics and politics of NGRS which unite NGR people all over the world, but they are not aware of their true ancestry, languages and culture.

The words Nigritian, Nigritia, Niger, Nigger and Negro have been handed to the present generation with all kinds of confusing definitions and connotations. I believe that it is through linguistics and history that we will expose the truth. In this work, the misinformation regarding the root word NGR and the word Nigger has been unmasked. The myth passed down to generations regarding the origin of the word Niger as a Latin word has been exploded. According to Dr. Ernie Smith, a professor of linguistics, the root word NGR is found in the Nigritian ancestors' languages. It was Dr. Smith who revealed to me that, while the word Niger entered into the English language via Latin and other Romance languages, the European lexicographers admit that the word Niger is not originally a Latin word. The American Heritage lexicographers openly declare the origin of the word Niger to be unknown to them.

I maintain that it is the root word NGR that is the tie that binds all NGRS together as one people. Most archeologists, anthropologists and scientists, refer to Nigritic people as being the original people in many ancient civilizations. We can start from the cradle of man and follow the Nile out of Africa to many civilizations as Nigritians spread across this planet. I maintain that a proper understanding of the origin and TRUE meaning of the words Nigritia, Nigritic, Nigrito, Nigritian, Niger, Nigger, Negro, and Negre etc., will give children who are descendants of enslaved Niger-Congo Africans a reference point from which to start, when it comes to research on their history and ancestral identity.

Today, although there are many NGRS who are either unaware or ashamed of their NGR ancestry, there are descendants of ancient Nigritians who are very, very comfortable with their Nigritian (NGR) heritage. These descendants of NGR people have no problem referring to themselves as Negroes, Negrerie, Nigritian, Nigerians, and Niggers. In fact, currently, there are references on various maps of Africa that identify NGR people where they live today. For example, there are the Nyangara or Ninagara people of East Africa. These NGR people's homeland is located on the border of Uganda and Sudan.

I should stress here also that there are many Nigritic people around the world who *are* aware of their ancient NGR ancestors. Like President Leopold Senghor, they too are striving to have the ancient name Nigritia used as a name for the entire continent known today as Africa.

Chapter Ten

THE N-WORD

In essence, it is my contention that the so-called N-word is not the problem. The ignorance of the true etymology of the so-called "N-word", coupled with the relentless vilification, the vicious distortions, and the continuous brainwashing against the N-word is the problem. There is a malicious intent and crusade at work to distort and destroy a royal regal people's Nigritian ancestral identity. The root word NGR, from its beginning, has a divine, spiritual and noble meaning.

Many black people tend to believe the lies that some European scholars have propagandized. Some black people believe that the definition of Nigger in some English dictionaries reflect, describe or prescribe their character. Those who believe such lies have bought into the doctrine of European white supremacy. In their uninformed embrace of this negative propaganda, they remain a prisoner within their own ignorance. Many Nigritic people embrace this distorted information, and false hypotheses without linguistic empirical documentation, or solid scientific research. Some African-American leaders have called for the removal of the word Nigger from dictionaries. If this happens, a link to Nigritian history will disappear. Knowledge is the key to destroy the negative connotation surrounding the name Nigger. We should educate the people about the word Nigger, not eradicate it. Accurate information regarding the root word NGR will take the negative power out of the name Nigger. It will put spirituality back into the name Nigger as it was in the beginning.

The distortion of the word Nigger became widely circulated with the invention of the modern day dictionary. During that time in history, Nigritians (Ngrs) were held in captivity/slavery under European domination. In order to justify the injustices and the inhuman treatment of Nigritian people, the process to demonize them as less then human began. The word Nigger happens to have been a vehicle in which to achieve this victory. The name Nigger has become entrenched as something negative within the mental psychic of both black and white people. Today, many black people cringe when the word Nigger is mentioned. They become highly indignant and angry when the name is applied to them. Some white people use the word Nigger to inflict psychological and mental abuse. They use it as a weapon, a form of psychological warfare. They seem to be winning. But there are Nigritians who embrace the name Nigger. They have knowledge of the origin of the name Nigger. They know that the name has a divine origin, and they are proud of their history.

Black and white people have been bamboozled. Again, Nigger has a negative connotation in the

European languages but it has a positive connotation in Nigritian languages. From its very beginning, Nigger has a divine origin. As we have discussed in this book, the ancient Egyptian language is part of the Nigritian family of languages. Today, the root NGR can be found inscribed on pyramids and temples throughout ancient Egypt. These hieroglyphic inscriptions of (NGR) stand as undeniable, irrefutable evidence that the word 'nigger' is not of Latin origin, but rather, of a divine Nigritian Kemetic origin. To the ancient Kemetic scribes, NGR referred to gods and goddesses.

In our continuing quest to recover and reconstruct our true Nigritian (African) history, one giant step is to debunk the prevailing, negative definition and usage of the word 'nigger'. We must strip it of its negative connotation and power by using it as a term of endearment. By redefining it and reclaiming it, we will begin the process of elevating it to its original divine meaning.

Visual 1

"The Goodess Hathor protecting the Pharaoh Psammetichus. The Goddess is represented as a cow, her sacred animal, with the solar disk the solar disk and the uraeus between her horns. A protector and nourisher of the living..." (Visual 1) New Larousse Encyclopedia Of Mythology 1968:47

Visual 2

"A sistrum-sharped column in the shrine of Hathor at Deir el-Bahri." "The Goddess Hathor is seen her with her characteristic cow ears. (visual 2) is from Hathor Rising, Roberts, Alison 1997:43"

NIGITA BEFORE EUROPEAN
SUPREMACY ABOUT 1815

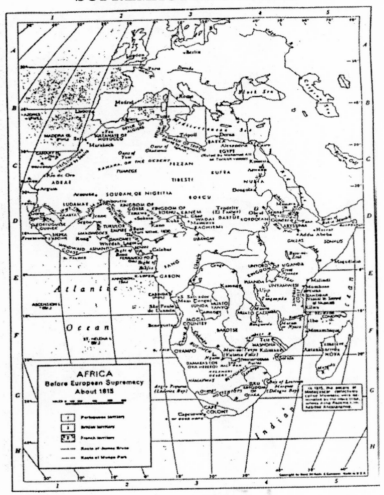

Visual 3
Map of Africa before European Supremacy about 1815[1]

---

[1] Rand McNally Atlas of World History, Edited by R.R. Palmer p.137

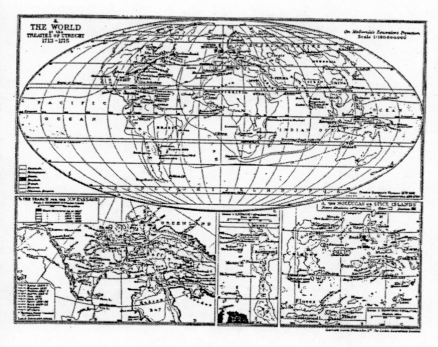

Visual 4

Muri's Ancient Atlas, and The London Geographical Institute

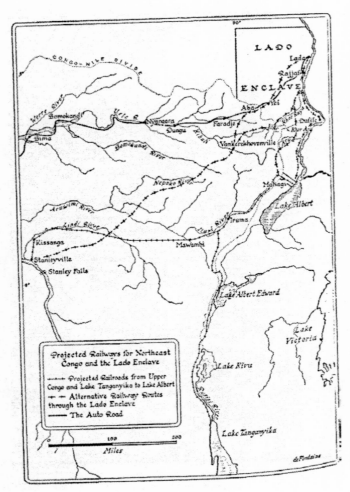

Visual 5

This map highlights Nyangara people located in the Enclave of Lado.[2]

---

[2] King Leopold, England & the Upper Nile 1899 – 1909, Collins, Robert O., Yale 1968

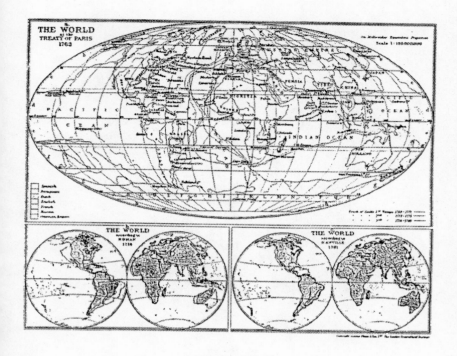

Visual 6

Muri's Ancient Atlas, And The London Geographical Institute.

NAGARI 1.

अ	आ	इ	ई	उ	उ	ऋ	ॠ
a	â	i	î	u	û	ri	rî
ऌ	ॡ	ए	ऐ	ओ	औ	अं	अः
lri	lri	e	ai	ô	ow	am	ah

क	ख	ग	घ	ङ
ka	kha	ga	gha	nga
च	छ	ज	झ	ञ
cha	chha	ja	jha	nya
ट	ठ	ड	ढ	ण
ta	tha	da	dha	na
त	थ	द	ध	न
ta	tha	da	dha	na
प	फ	ब	भ	म
pa	pha	ba	bha	ma
य	र	ल	व	
ya	ra	la	va	
श	ष	स	ह	क्ष
sa	sha	sa	ha	ksha

NAGARI 1

Visual 7

Devanagari (Nagari)

Devanagari (Nagari) is the name given to the character in which Sanskrit is generally written, especially in northern and middle India. The Indus commonly employ the second term rather than the first ... Devanagari (Nagari) signfies "(writing) of the divine city." The New International Encyclopaedia, 1927:736, Nagari Alphbet, Fry, Edmound, Pantographia, Containing Accurate copies Of All The Known Alphabets in the World; Together with An English Explanation of The Peculair Force or Power Of Each Letter, :206)

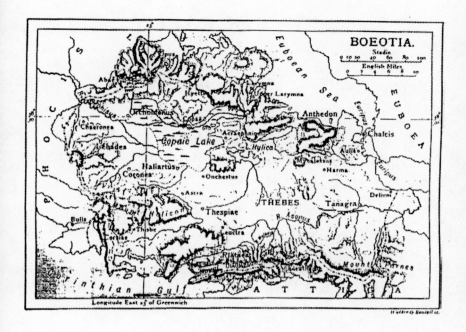

Visual 8

A copy of this map is found in <u>A History Of Greece To The Death Of Alexander The Great</u>, Bury, J.B., 1917:162

BIBLIOGRAPHY

Baines, John. Conceptions of God in Ancient Egypt, The One And The Many, Cornell University Press, 1982.

Birch, Samuel. Introduction To The Study Of The Egyptian Hieroglyphs, Bradbury And Evans, Printers Black World, 1971.

Breasted, James H. A History Of Egypt, Bantam Book, New York, Toronto, London, 1967.

Budge, E.A.Wallis. The Gods Of The Egyptians, Volume I, II, Dover Publishers, Inc., 31 East 2nd Street, Mineola, N.Y. 11501, 1969.

Budge, E.A. Wallis. An Egyptian Hieroglyphic Dictionary, Volume I, II, Dover Publications, Inc., New York, 1978

Budge, E.A.Wallis. Babylonian Life and History, Cooper Square Publishers, Inc., New York, 1975.

Bury, J.B. D.Litt. A History Of Greece To The Death Of Alexander The Great, Macmillan And Co., Limited St. Martin's Street, London 1917.

Cleugh, James. The Crescent and the Bull, Translated from German Hawthorne Books, Inc, New York.

Collins, Roberts O. King Leopold, England & the Upper Nile 1899 – 1909, Yale 1968.

Durant, Will. Our Oriental Heritage, Simon And Schuster, New York, 1954.

Foner, Philip S. Dr. W.E.B. DUBOIS Speaks, Pathfinder, New York, London, Sydney, Toronto, 1970.

Fry, Edmound. Pantographia: Accurate Copies of All The Known Alphabets In The World, Coopers and Wilson, London.

Gay Robins. Women in Ancient Egypt, Harvard University Press Cambridge, Massachusetts, 1993.

Gerald Massey. Ancient Egypt The Light Of The World Volume I, II, Black Classic Press, P.O. Box 13414, Baltimore, MD 21203, 1992.

Gerald Massey. Book Of The Beginnings, Volume I, II, Noble Offset Printing Inc., New York, N.Y., 1974.

Hughes, Langston & Meltzer, Milton. A Pictorial History of the Negro In America, Crown Publishers, Inc., New York, N.Y.

New Age Bible Interpretation Old Testament Volume III, New Age Press, Oceanside, California 92054, 1955.

New Larousse Encyclopedia of Mythology, Crescent Books, New York, 1987.

Herrmann, Paul. Translated from the German by Michael Bulloch, Conquest by Man, by Harper & Brothers, Publishers, New York, 1954.

Rand McNally, Atlas of World History, Edited by R.R. Palmer, Rand McNally & Company, New York, Chicago, San Francisco.

Roberts, Alison. Hathor Rising, Inner Traditions International, One Park Street, Rochester, Vermont, 1997.

Sellassie, Sergew, Hable. Ancient and Medieval Ethiopian History to 1270, United Printer Addis Adaba, Ethiopia, 1972.

Sertima Van, Ivan. Black Women In Antiquity, 1990.

Spence Lewis. Ancient Egyptian Myths And Legends, Dover Publications, Inc., New York, 1990.

The New International Encyclopaedia, Volume VI, Dodd, Mead And Company, New York, 1927.

Walker, Barbara G. The Woman's Dictionary of Symbols & Sacred Objects, Harper & Row Publisher, San Francisco.

Walker, Barbara G. The Woman's Encyclopedia of Myths and Secrets, Harper San Francisco, A Division of Harper Collins Publishers, 1983.

Wallbank, Walter T. and Taylor, Alstair M. Civilization—Past and Present, Volume I, Scott, Foresman And Company, Chicago, Atlanta, Dallas, New York, 1942.

Welch, G. North African Prelude, The First Seven Thousands Years, William Morrow and Company, New York, 1949.

Illustration Acknowledgments

Bury, J.B. A History OF Greece To The Death Of Alexander The Great, Macmillan and Co, Limited St Martin Street, London, 1917:162.

Collins, Robert O. King Leopold, England & The Upper Nile 1899 – 1909, Yale 1968.

Fry, Edmound. Pantographia, Containing Accurate copies Of All The Known Alphabets in the World; Together with An English Explanation of The Peculiar Force or Power Of Each Letter, Cooper and Wilson, 206.

Muri's Ancient Atlas, and The London Geographical Institute.

New Larousse Encyclopedia Of Mythology, Crescent Books, New York, 1987:47.

Palmer, R.R., Rand McNally Atlas Of World History, Rand McNally & Company, New York, Chicago, San Francisco, p. 137.

Roberts, Alison. Hathor Rising The Power Of The Goddess In Ancient Egypt, Inner Traditions International, Rochester, Vermont, 1997:43.

Write Down What You Have Learned!

Write Down What You Have Learned!

Write Down What You Have Learned!

Write Down What You Have Learned!

Write Down What You Have Learned!

Write Down What You Have Learned!

Write Down What You Have Learned!

Write Down What You Have Learned!

Write Down What You Have Learned!

Write Down What You Have Learned!

Write Down What You Have Learned!

Write Down What You Have Learned!

Write Down What You Have Learned!

Write Down What You Have Learned!

Write Down What You Have Learned!

Write Down What You Have Learned!

Write Down What You Have Learned!

Write Down What You Have Learned!

Write Down What You Have Learned!

Write Down What You Have Learned!

Write Down What You Have Learned!

Order Form

Milligan Books, Inc.

1425 W. Manchester Ave., Suite C, Los Angeles, CA 90047

(323) 750-3592

Name_____ Date _____

Address _____

City_____ State____ Zip Code _____

Day Telephone _____

Evening Telephone_____

Book Title_____

Number of books ordered___ Total ....$ _____

Sales Taxes (CA Add 8.25%) ....$ _____

Shipping & Handling $4.90 for one book..$ _____

Add $1.00 for each additional book...........$ _____

Total Amount Due.....................................$ _____

☐ Check ☐ Money Order ☐ Other Cards _____

☐Visa ☐ MasterCard Expiration Date _____

Credit Card No. _____

Driver License No. _____

Make check payable to Milligan Books, Inc.

_____   _____

Signature   Date

Printed in the United States
1386900008B/1-66